D0940675

Mother's Hour

Books by Mrs. White

Mother's Faith

For the Love of Christian Homemaking

Early Morning Revival Challenge

Mother's Book of Home Economics

Living on His Income

Old Fashioned Motherhood

Economy for the Christian Home

Mother's Hour

[Cover photo: A Parlour Table in Mrs. White's Vermont home]

Mother's Hour

Encouragement from Home for the Christian Housewife

The Legacy of Home Press
puritanlight@gmail.com

Mother's Hour
Copyright 2015 by Mrs. Sharon White
All Rights Reserved

The content of this book is gathered from previously published posts from
The Legacy of Home blog, and "Letters from the Estate" private
newsletters, written by Mrs. Sharon White. These were originally
published during the years of 2013 to 2015.

No portion of this book may be copied without permission from the
publisher.

The Legacy of Home Press
ISBN-13: 978-0692579978
ISBN-10: 0692579974
Mother's Hour
Author - Mrs. Sharon White

Contents

Mother's Hour

Introduction

There used to be radio programs called, "Gospel Hour" and "The Hymn – Singing Hour" which were a great blessing to many of the Lord's people. They would pause from their work and sit by the radio to hear the spiritual nourishment. Sometimes they only had a few minutes to spare. Perhaps they only heard the end of the program, or a few minutes in the middle, but this was enough to get them back to a joyful state of mind doing the great work of the Lord in their daily lives.

Mother's Hour is designed to be a time of refreshment, a time to stop and read a sort of modern day radio program. It contains domestic writings for mothers, wives, and grandmothers. The author wrote these from her home in rural Vermont. Here she shares some of her life as a Christian Housewife. These are like devotionals; some are brief while others are longer. These writings were mostly gleaned from a private monthly newsletter ("Letters from the Estate") sent to subscribers by "old fashioned" mail. The rest were taken from her blog, "The Legacy of Home."

Whether you have a few minutes or an entire hour to sit and read, it is the hope of the publisher that you will find encouragement for your work in a Christian Home.

1

Setting up Housekeeping

I have been reading about the life of Mamie Eisenhower. She was an army wife who moved many times. She lived abroad and in the United States. One way she made each place feel like home was by painting her bedroom the exact same color wherever she lived. She would keep a paint card to help her locate the right shade. Her room was always a "moss green" with pink curtains. There were times she had to move again right after she settled in the last place. Her trick for making the new place feel like home was by immediately putting up paintings and family portraits on the walls. She would also roll out carpet (like oriental rugs) to make the place look homey.

When she was a young wife, her mother would give her gifts of place settings and table linens for birthdays and holidays. Slowly she acquired enough to be a "good hostess." She always welcomed guests in her home, as well as soldiers who worked with her husband, and their wives.

She was a frugal shopper who often made use of storage units to store items which she could not take overseas. These items of "home" were there when she returned to the states to set up a new, temporary, residence in the U.S. She, and her husband Dwight, did not purchase their own home until just before he became President of the United States. She was in her 50's at the time.*

As my children become settled in homes of their own, there are certain basic things they need to set up the new house. These include dishes, wash cloths, towels, bedding, silverware, cooking and baking pans. They also need a kitchen table, a comfortable chair, a bed, lamps and a bureau. As time goes on, more things can be acquired – such as a sofa and bookcases.

(It used to be that an iron and ironing board were essential. These items are in every hotel room, but are not common in the homes of the younger generation. Still, they would make a lovely gift.)

To start out with, they usually have some pretty picture on the wall with a Bible verse or prayer in nice lettering. From there they can find artwork as they go along, visiting thrift stores, yard sales, or stores. This helps them learn to decorate with their own style.

We usually have a set of "starter silverware" which is very inexpensive. Eventually, they can replace this with a better set, or we can give them one as a birthday gift. Buying a pretty tea cup, tea kettle, set of mixing bowls, bread knife, or a nice little painting are lovely gifts to help someone set up their home.

Little domestic gifts inspire the homemaker to clean, decorate, and keep things looking lovely. I have many things that were given to me from the homes of family members. I have a white lamp decorated with roses. There are charming paintings, and pieces of furniture from the homes of relatives. These are my most cherished possessions. Giving items from our own possessions to help set up the homes of our children and grandchildren is a wonderful way to help them start out in life.

* Mamie and Dwight arranged to have their new home blessed by the Reverend Elson. Here is his prayer:

"Bless this house, that it may henceforth be a place of health and healing, a haven of tranquility, an abode of love, and a sanctuary of worship. Bless all who call it home, and all the loved ones and friends who are encompassed by it in abiding love and devotion to Thee."

- From "Mrs. Ike: Memories and Reflections on the life of Mamie Eisenhower" by her granddaughter, Susan.

Mother's Hour

2

Treasures from the Museum

There is a historical society and museum in our small village town. It is housed in an old schoolhouse just down the road. All summer long the museum is open for a couple of hours one day a week. There is, however, an annual event that attracts the community to attend. It is a fundraiser / yard sale. The merchandise is donated by the residents of our town and surrounding communities.

This yearly event is a wonderful time to see and visit with our neighbors and to look around the museum.

It happened a few weeks ago. John (18) was my escort. (He is also a wonderful bodyguard, since he is a foot taller than me, and a carrier of heavy parcels.) I loved looking at all the antique items in the building. I saw many treasures that I am sure homemakers in the area generously parted with.

I found a few low cost items and had John carry them home for me. I bought two sets of ruffled curtains for 50 cents each: A small white set for my kitchen, and a pink one for the children's nursery on the main floor of our estate. I also found many wooden paintings with charming illustrations of children's scenes for the walls of the nursery. Each cost 25 cents. I also bought a box full of beautiful dishes with a delicate rose pattern. The cost was $3 for the entire box. When I got home, I found that the box contained a wonderful surprise. It was a vintage homemaker's apron and is just lovely!

I washed the curtains, put them up on the widows, and had someone arrange the paintings on the walls of the nursery. Once everything was in order, I went back to my usual homemaking duties.

Each time I had a guest in the house, I had such fun presenting the paintings, curtains, and dishes by saying, "I got these from a Museum." It sounds so much more fun than saying, "I got these from a yard sale!"

- One must find one's fun whenever the situation arises. -

3

Living on Less

I am often hearing the younger generation complain that the current minimum wage, at $9 an hour, is not enough. They gripe and complain that it is not fair and they deserve more. When I hear this, I can't help talking about the Great Depression and how people were grateful to even have a job, often working for food or a dollar a day! In response, I get that look, as if I am saying that I had to walk five miles to school in the middle of a snowstorm every day of my childhood. It is amusing.

The problem today is not just that people want money to spend on luxuries; they want to live well above their means. They want many things *right now* and often credit cards and subsequent debt help them to "succeed." But they need more than $9 an hour to pay for this way of life. Sadly, the culture around us has taught that this is considered a basic standard of living.

In the early 1990's, when my husband and I had three small children, minimum wage was $5 an hour. I remember our tiny 3 bedroom apartment, right down the street from a Massachusetts beach.

There was no such thing as cell phones or computers. There were no cell phone bills or internet plans. We did not have credit cards or debt. We lived a very simple life. We had enough money to pay our small rent, utilities, gasoline for the car, and humble food. We did not have money for gifts, shopping, clothing, eating out, or spending money. We made the best of what we had.

When extra money came in from overtime, tax refunds, or some other way, we were *very grateful*. This was what we used to purchase what we lacked. Still, we had to be creative. There were small thrift stores in our area and annual sales at the local Sears Roebuck store. Like the mothers before me, I made sure my children looked nice, as I chose pretty and practical dresses for my girls, and nice overalls and handsome clothes for my boys, even if I had to make some of them myself. (Being "poor" did not lower our level of cleanliness or proper manners.)

For entertainment, we read library books, took walks to the playground and beach, and visited our extended family. An invitation for dinner at the homes of relatives was much more fun than eating at any restaurant could ever be.

We used to write letters because we could not afford long distance phone calls. Some of our family lived outside our area - code even though they were in the same state. We had to limit those phone calls, talking briefly, and always watching the clock for fear of a high bill.

We bought an old car for a few hundred dollars. The windows were often stuck and we could not open the passenger door. When we all went out together, my husband would hand me one child at a time, through the window, and I would buckle them into the back carseats. The car was safe, it ran well, but it was beat up. My husband and his friends used their own labor to keep it running, even if that often meant "duct tape" repairs. We were grateful for transportation that we could afford. If the car broke down, we walked or took the bus until we had enough money to get it fixed. I have often walked a few miles, with a radio flyer wagon, to grocery shop with small children.

Perhaps the reason we managed so well, living on less, *and were happy*, was because we knew no other way. This is something the rising generation needs to experience.

4

I Cannot Do It All

The weather here at the Estate is lovely. Mister has painted one of our picnic tables and it helps make the front property look fresh and new. He also helped me plant cucumbers in a small front garden. Our strawberry plants are thriving up on the hill. This is our third year as amateur gardeners.

Each day I open the windows and put potted flowers on the sills. I have daises, mini roses, white flowers and purple ones. These are all on the second floor and as I look at them, I can see the lower landscape of the property. It reminds me of a cozy apartment where window boxes and patio gardens are common. It is a touch of home that anyone can have.

Mother's Hour

I have vacuumed and swept and polished the rooms. I vacuumed the front staircase and cleaned the entryway. I have done laundry and dishes. I have baked and cooked, and took time to enjoy my pretty flowers. Then one day, not too long ago, my glasses went missing. I am always losing them. But this time, someone accidentally stepped on them. I normally use them to read and to drive. I also like to wear them when I clean so I can see all the crumbs and messes, to make everything look sparkling and nice.

So this past week, with my impaired vision, I have learned another needed lesson. I cannot do it all. Others have stepped in, and life has been more leisurely. I still clean and cook, but others are doing some of the sweeping and washing. Others are doing all the driving. I was clearing off the table and doing dishes and one of the children said, "Mom, how can you still clean when you can't see?" I told her that I had everything just about memorized and it was a habit to just keep working.

The laundry and the housework are a basic part of my daily life. But when I cannot see the jelly grandbaby has gotten on the floor, someone gets the mop and washes it all up. I only notice it when I step on it. But someone comes along and gets it clean. (gentle smiles)

Because I cannot see very well, I am more quiet. It has dimmed one of the senses that keep one on alert and overly busy. I work at a gentler pace and the family has been sweet about this, my latest handicap.

Soon I will have a new pair of glasses. They have been ordered. The money has come as a blessing from the Lord. A donation came the day before the glasses broke. I am taken care of by my precious Lord before a need has even happened.

I am thankful to learn that others come around me and help me through this life; Even if this is just in housework and errands. If you notice this post has typing errors, please understand. I have the keyboard memorized, but can't see well enough to fix my mistakes. That is just like my life I suppose, flawed despite my best efforts.

5

Pleasant Hours of Housework

I was reading a bit from "Farmer Boy," by Laura Ingalls Wilder. I had already cleaned the parlour, swept the floors and did some dishes. I had fed grandbaby and settled him down for his nap. As I read, I was intrigued and inspired by how Ma and Pa Wilder industriously kept the farm.

There was certain heavy work that happened at specific seasons. Ice was carved out and stacked in the ice house. This was the main work at hand, for days, in addition to daily chores. When the men finished with this, the ice was all set for the coming year.

Later, in springtime, the maple trees were tended to. Here in Vermont, this is a common event. Much of life stops while the sap is "running." The sap is gathered and boiled and processed. For Mother Wilder, much of it became cakes of maple sugar. The rest was saved in jugs as the year's supply of syrup!

Oh, then it was time for the entire house to be cleaned! The carpets were un-tacked and taken outside to be cleaned. The rooms were emptied and washed and scrubbed! They were also whitewashed and made ready for the next season.

While Pa worked with the fields, in his workshop, in the barns, and kept busy with his chores. Ma made large, delicious meals and kept a lovely home. Ma also had a workroom where she kept a loom and made the family's clothes!

Well, this all got me thinking. . . And all I wanted to do was dust the house, sweep the rooms and vacuum the carpets! I wanted to wash windows and then take a little rest before I started the great task of preparing the evening meal. These were just little jobs. These are jobs that are re-done on a regular basis. But as each task is "done," there is a sense of pride for the hard work being accomplished to make home a happy, special place.

These are the pleasant hours we spend at home, doing the housework.

6

Bedtime at the Estate

The sun had gone down. The grandchildren had their baths - the toddler and the newborn. John (16) and I scurried around doing dishes and cleaning the parlour. All the children's toys and clothing from the day were put away. The last of the laundry was finished and we tucked in all the kitchen chairs.

"It is almost bedtime. . ." I called out to one of the children. I shut off the bright lights and turned on some dim lamps. This is part of the signal to quiet down the day. A nice cup of milk and a blanket and pillow were prepared for the toddler. He lay down happily and was quiet in his little bed. The newborn went off with mother. The house was quiet and peaceful.

John and I sat at the table and did our Bible time.

Soon it was time for we grownups to go to sleep. It had been such a long day, with so much work - laughter and noise! We had cleaned and cooked and worked here at the Estate. We were tired.

I love that children have their own bedtimes. We adults work very hard watching over them and tending them. It is good for them to have a routine of baths and quiet and snuggling up in their little beds. We parents need to have our own peaceful, evening routines after the young ones are asleep.

While we do not always get every bit of the day's work finished here, I love to take one last glance back over the rooms before the last light goes out. It is a moment of gratefulness for all we have, and I am able to rest content in our happy home.

Mother's Hour

7

Nobody Wants to Clean a Messy House

Cleaning to me is part of decorating. I go through the house and tidy things up and make them look pleasant to the eyes. Home decorating is a way to create a nice atmosphere for the family. This is done without money. It is done every day when the chairs are made neat and pillows are fluffed. It is when furniture polish makes surfaces bright and gleaming in the afternoon sun. It creates an ambiance.

I clean throughout the day, or else things will get out of control. I clean whenever I see something out of place, as I walk by the way. (Of course, stopping at a certain hour to end the day's work and enjoy some leisurely rest.) I clean a neat home, but of course the work is a little harder at mealtime when the most work is needed to be done.

But nobody wants to clean a mess.

We have all walked into an unattended kitchen and seen spills and crumbs and dishes all over the place. This is a messy mess and no one wants to go in there. Very often this happens when it has been left to the care of children or teenagers. They just don't have the experience to keep things nice and keep messes decent.

We have also seen a child's bedroom that looked like a tornado had been there. No housekeeper would walk in there without sighing. This is not a pleasant type of cleaning! So we call in the child and we put them through a training session. I love to make these humorous. I will say to the child, "I wonder what happened in here?" To which the child will shrug and look around to survey the damage. It is almost like the child was oblivious to the mess until mother pointed it out. I smile and say, "Well, let's clean this together." Do you know why I don't demand the child do it alone? Because that would be unfair and too much. It is obvious that help is needed to get things under control. I also use this time to re-teach how to do the work. And lecture about cleanliness. This not only gets the message through, but sometimes bores the child so much they would rather have the room kept clean than have mother talk about cleaning for hours! (gentle smiles)

I will show the child how to make the bed by taking all the bedding and throw it on the floor. I will put on a sheet, arrange the pillow and make the bed. I will talk while I do it, as if I am sharing how to make a meal from a recipe. When it looks nice and neat, I will say something like, "See? Doesn't that look better?" When the child's face brightens (probably because he thinks he got out of making his own bed), I will say, "Now it's your turn." I will take all the bedding and throw it back on the floor. Then I will watch and direct while the child remakes his own bed.

Mother's Hour

Next we go to the bureau drawers. I start with one drawer. We sort the junk from the clothes and fold and make things neat. Then I take it all back out and put it on the floor. The child redoes each drawer on his own, just like we made the bed.

We go on to the bookcase, the floor, and all through the room until I have shown how to clean it all, and the child has redone my work.

Granted, I must have time to do all this, and it only happens a couple of times a year. But once the training session is done, that child does not want to hear me say, on another day, "Hey, do you want me to help you clean your room?" (smiles) Because now they have learned that it is quicker and easier to just do it on their own.

We can do this with any room in the house - the kitchen, the living room. We can re-do jobs with the children until they are ready to take on the chores responsibly and on their own. Children should be taught to spend between one and two hours a day in personal cleanliness and chores. This is something they will have to do all through their lives.

However, sometimes when we mothers are too overwhelmed, sick, or tired, we might just walk into one of those messy rooms, sigh, and say we will work on it later. We will just have to make that mess look pretty, rest up, and then get the help from the family to retrain and make the home look nice again.

This, of course, is the training ground for children to gain an excellent work ethic. These skills we teach, to have a clean home where their own labor made it happen, is what helps build character.

8

The Ceremony of Breakfast

I was thinking how nice it would be to have a supply of linen tablecloths and napkins. These can be used to set a formal table each morning. The table could have a fresh cloth spread over it in the evening, before retiring for the night, so it is ready for morning. (Perhaps I can find some at thrift stores and consignment shops?)

A saucer could hold an upside down teacup at each place setting. This is the way an elegant table is set. When a guest sits at his place, he simply turns the cup upright for his coffee or tea. Nice silverware should be at each place. This should include a spoon, fork, and butter knife, along with a linen napkin.

One could set out a small tray of assorted teabags, and possibly packages of instant oatmeal. A hot pot of boiling water in a pretty kettle could be placed on a "trivet" in the center of the table, for the hostess to serve younger guests. Adults and teenagers can certainly serve themselves as they are seated around the table. A container of creamer (or milk) could be set near the kettle, along with a sugar bowl.

The breakfast can include a basket holding fresh baked rolls, biscuits, quick bread, or muffins. These should be placed inside a linen cloth and covered with another cloth to keep them fresh and warm. One would also need a plate of butter near the basket.

A nice bowl of freshly cut fruit, or whole fruit, would be nice to go along with the meal. Each place should also have a small cup for orange juice.

The breakfast menu can be anything from eggs, fried potatoes, toast, and grapefruit to blueberry pancakes and syrup. Some families would have a boiled egg with toast and fruit each morning before heading off to work or school. If there is not much time, a light meal of cereal can go well with the fresh fruit and muffins.

Each of us should be sure to dress and be ready for the day before coming to the table.

The entire ceremony of setting a breakfast table and having all come to sit together in the morning can become the foundation of manners and endearing fellowship. Taking the time to eat real, nourishing food all together would be good for our health. This is a time for the "morning nourishment" which can begin and end with a precious prayer. I cannot think of a better way to start the day in a lovely, pleasant way.

9

Time with Mister

One of the grown children called in the early evening. He just finished his shift at work and had locked the keys in his car. Could someone come by with a spare set and help? We looked out the window. It was not quite 5 o'clock. It was dark and snow was falling. The streets were slippery. Mister offered to drive. I went along for the ride.

Rural Vermont in the winter is a beautiful, peaceful place to be. I find it very restful when Mister does the driving. I can sit and enjoy the snowy landscape. Mister often reaches out to hold my hand as he drives along. He lets me listen to what I like on the car radio. At this time of year, Christmas music is playing continuously on our local station.

When we arrived at our destination, Mister got out and cleaned off our son's car. The door was opened with the spare key, and the engine was started to warm it up. I watched the two of them under a lamplight, talking, as snow fell all around them. I was thankful to be in a warm, cozy car.

As we drove back home, it was pleasant and quiet. I remembered our last outing, when we dropped off one of the vehicles for repairs early one morning. The drive home with Mister is always special because it doesn't happen very often.

In almost 3 decades of marriage, we have never had a "night out." We never went on a "date." It is not something we ever thought about. Our time outside the home or family was always practical. Our outings are essential errands. They have always been that way.

During these drives, we don't argue. We don't talk about any worries or problems because they don't enter our minds. We enjoy the car ride and the beauty around us. Mister makes sure the car heat is warm enough for me, and that I am comfortable. He opens the door for me and makes sure I am safe. These gentlemanly acts of kindness are what make the trips a little respite from the trials of life.

We are also very grateful when we arrive safely back at home. Despite our flaws and normal annoyances in daily life, we have work

Mother's Hour

to do. It does not matter that we are both worn out. Our children and grandchildren need us. They need us to stand strong - together- and get back to the business at hand - the striving and cultivating of a godly lighthouse, despite a cold, imperfect world.

10

Baking in the Kitchen

You would not believe how moody I get if I inadvertently step away from the Spiritual warmth of the fire. In other words, if I do not consistently listen to sermons, old time gospel music, and read spiritually edifying literature on a regular basis, I get cold and unhappy. Why? Because the world seeps in. The hurricanes of our cultures' troubles overwhelm me. The normal drama of family life and the flaws of human nature make me sad. This happened to me for a few days recently. I was easily irritated, and easily brought to tears. It was time to sort through my stack of sermons on CD, listen to them, and get back to my usual reading of the likes of "The Sword of the Lord" newspaper, which is full of old time sermons and wonderful godly writings.

It was also time to get back into the kitchen. I got out some cookbooks and looked for a nice recipe for coffee cake. I put on my apron, turned on our charming kitchen lamp and got to work. As I gathered the tools and ingredients (flour, mixing bowl, measuring cup, etc.), I felt such peace. I put time and love into my baking, and my happiness returned. I was listening to Bing Crosby, on my kitchen radio, as he sang Christmas songs. This made me think of family, and holiday cooking. It was inspiring.

As I took the cake out of the oven, I noticed the time. It was 10 p.m. I did not realize it was way past my bedtime. But it was all worth it. In just a few short hours of listening to sermons, reading good literature, and doing some precious homemaking, my joy had returned.

Snowy Days at Our Vermont Estate

Grandbaby and I went on a horse-drawn carriage ride this weekend. We had the Uncles with us. "The Uncles" are my sons John (16) and Matt (20). Uncle Matt wore his wool overcoat and a pair of sunglasses. He looked charming. He held baby. Baby loves both of his Uncles, but when there are difficult things to do, Uncle Matt is the one baby reaches for. He held baby and comforted him during the entire ride. Baby felt safe and secure and very happy.

It is cozy here at home. Our wood stove is blazing and the gospel music is playing quietly in the background. We will make a small batch of sugar cookies late this afternoon.

It can get bitterly cold here with temperatures below zero. We have to close up some of the house to maintain heat in only a few of the rooms. Our parlour is the main room where we keep it mostly cozy. It is attached to our kitchen. We put up a pretty floral quilt in the hall doorway to block out any cold drafts. It makes things look vintage and old fashioned to have a curtain - of - sorts for a door!

Mothers in the old days would stuff newspapers in windowsills and cracks in the walls to help keep out the chill. Can you imagine how cold it must have been (before modern heating and plumbing) when families would wake up and find a sheet of ice over the water in a washbasin on cold winter mornings?

With heating costs so high, we have to work on overcoming depression and sadness on the coldest of days. We have to bundle up and think of our extra efforts at warmth as an adventure! We may notice the pretty snow outside and decide to make a hot cup of tea or hot chocolate to provide an extra sense of comfort and warmth. Knitting or crocheting by the fire (or electric heater) are nice ways to stay warm. If one can bake or cook something special, it will certainly help heat up the kitchen. It is good to set a "mood" or create an "ambiance" of *home*.

I love having a little lamp in my kitchen. It adds a sense of gentleness to our evenings. In just a little while, I will wash dishes and start supper. Grandbaby will sit in his highchair and play while I work. I will give him little treats and little toys as I go along. Then baby and I will sit by the window and look at the snowy landscape and enjoy the view from the second story of this 1800's Estate. It shall be another pleasant day in Vermont.

12

Family Life in the Old Days

Lately, I have been noticing a major shift in society. It has become common that expectant mothers are seeking out daycares for when their babies are born. It has become normal to place children into centers and private homes to take care of babies and small children until they are old enough to go to school.

This is all part of the emptying of homes and the breakdown of the close, traditional family. I understand there are those in very difficult circumstances who have no choice. But it should not be the normal way for everyone to live. It is not possible that every family is in such a crisis that children must be away from their mothers, and away from their homes, for much of their childhoods.

In my generation, we children had the security of nice neighborhoods where housewives were at home. We children played in the yards and walked to the beaches, parks, and the little corner stores. We went home before the streetlights came on in summer evenings. While we never strayed far from our houses, we were generally in earshot of our mothers in case they called us home. Sometimes a neighbor Mother might see us at the private beach down the road from our house, and she might call over and say, "Your mother just called. She needs you at home." We respected all the families in our community. It was all family - oriented rather than career oriented - or materialistic. The families lived simply in older homes and no one had more than one television set. (gentle smiles).

In our schools, I never saw a sick child. Mothers would keep children at home so as not to spread germs. If a teacher noticed a child seemed the slightest bit ill in our schools, she would send him to the nurse where he was promptly sent home to his mother. Children were to rest, nursed by Mom, with hot soups, bed rest, and fluids. We children were kept in our beds in a loving, comforting version of a home hospital. Then we were able to get back to school and enjoy playing outdoors with the neighborhood children.

Today, I am noticing that more and more mothers are having trouble taking time off work to tend to their sick children. The children are then sent to school or daycare while they are contagious and this spreads more and more sickness and misery. It is a sad state to be in. It is very hard on everyone.

If only babies and little ones could stay at home under the loving, watchful care of their mothers. If only society had not changed so much to make it almost impossible to have an old - time family - life like in previous generations.

13

Housekeeping - With a Will

Duty is very difficult in a self - indulgent world. We wives often want to live in leisure, enjoy hobbies, and relax. Today, the American Dream is considered to be all about retirement! Yet, working in the home makes our surroundings pleasant, peaceful, and orderly. I recently heard the advice from a doctor (from a 1940's movie) suggesting to his nurse that an upper class housewife should let some of her servants go, do 6 hours of housework a day, and then her health would be recovered in 3 months!

"Duty with a will" means we have the right attitude of perseverance. We do the daily chores despite our mood or emotions. Often the task seems overwhelming and we have trouble even getting started. Perhaps we have neglected the deep-down cleaning for weeks or months. This becomes a mountain of impossibility! But with a will, we can take each step and work little-by-little to make things nice. Years ago, I read this old book about this young man who had to work in the fields. I can't remember all the details but I remember him saying to himself over and over again, *"With a will, Joe!"* And this became the motto of his life. He did his duties and he did them well.

One of the sweetest things I've found to help get that "will" strong, is to dress for the day in a housewife's uniform. This is a special outfit that says, "I am the hostess of this house and am happy to serve and make sure you are comfortable." For some this may be a little jewelry, a special hairstyle, a pretty dress and . . . of course . . . a pretty apron. This says that home is lovely and I am happy to work here.

Many mornings I have been giving myself little "pep talks" so I can drag myself out of bed. (gentle smiles) Life can get overwhelming and exhausting and we have to learn to do our very best, despite these challenges.

On a daily basis, grandbaby keeps me busy; my (mostly grown) children keep things exciting around here; and the care of my parents (the great-grandparents who live with us) have health issues which are a constant concern. I also am dealing with a gnawing disappointment I feel because I have not been able to knit an old fashioned sweater- and- bonnet set for my new grandbaby, who will arrive next month. Regardless of this, I still have a home to keep, a husband to care for, and plenty of work to do; I will not despair. I will do it, to the best of my ability, with a smile and *with a will.*

14

On the Edge of a Cliff

On a Friday afternoon, one of my boys needed my help. He was at the D.M.V. and needed to get his car registered before they closed. We had talked about this over the last few months. It had to get done, but for some reason he wasn't able to go until this "last minute." He was missing some paperwork and wondered if I would drive over there to meet him with the necessary documents.

My rushing to his aid made me think of helping a member of the family run for political office. Everyone jumps in there to do their part. Each helper will do even the smallest of tasks, despite weariness, to get that person elected to office. When one is surrounded by a family who is cheering them on, helping them finish a race, we are all excited when there is a victory.

Teaching young adults not to wait until the last minute to do basic things is an ongoing challenge for we mothers. I often say, "no more of this edge of the cliff requests, okay? I am getting old." (gentle smiles) But we must. We have to step in there when the situation calls for it.

When we know our child is doing his best, trying his hardest, but still gets into a situation that requires help, it is a blessing to step into action to help and encourage these young people into adulthood. They cannot do it alone.

We are the coaches and the cheerleaders in their young lives. We are the mentors. Someday, our children will become mentors to the next generation. Hopefully we will set a good example.

15

The House Coat

There is a sort of casualness in dress when at home. Many want to be comfortable when they are resting and relaxing. I like to wear a "house coat," especially in the winter. Here in New England, it is called a "robe." I first heard of the term "house coat," as a teenager when I was staying with my Alabama relatives. It was one of those culture shocks that took me awhile to adjust to. But it was adorable.

A "robe" seems very casual, but a "house coat" is more elegant. It is so easy to change our outlook with a simple saying.

Mother's Hour

I have this pretty purple robe. It is trimmed with embroidered, silvery, white snowflakes and has a zipper in the front. It looks like a traditional house robe that older women are known to wear. It is warm and pretty. There is a sense of dressing up, even while being casual at home.

My Aunt and Mother had similar house coats they wore at home. It gave us children a sense of security knowing that they were home with us. We knew that while they were in those pretty robes, doing housework, or sitting with us in the living room, they were not going anywhere. They were HOME.

Sometimes, if I have my coat on and my purse in hand, my little Grandson gets sad. He knows I am going out and he gets upset. But when he sees me in my house robe, he just smiles and goes about his day. He feels happy and secure that "Meme" is HOME.

16

It Is Not the Sabbath

Sometimes I complain to myself about all the work it takes to maintain and keep a home and family. This is normal murmuring, and human nature. But for me, it is not okay. We can all get used to being "normal" and accept our selfish, ease-seeking nature. I have also noticed this happening whenever I direct some extra housework to one of my teenagers. My child complains. He wants to know "why" he has to take the trash out, and couldn't it wait until he has another break? (gentle smiles)

This week, a wonderful thing happened. Whenever I heard a complaint about work, I would say, "Today is not the Sabbath." It is not our day of rest. While we most certainly can take breaks, and get our sleep at night, we have to work for 6 days. In this way, I am able to encourage myself and my children in Holy living. I bring the reality of God's laws into our daily life. It makes the chores and the work like mitzvahs * as we happily do things God's way.

This makes the Sabbath that much more of a wonderful, special day. It helps us to delight in the Lord and in our much earned reward . . . On the Sabbath, we get to rest!!

* *mitzvahs: Commandments and good deeds.*

17

All These Accomplishments

We have all heard of supermoms who have perfect homes and perfect families. They are "accomplished," which means they have many skills. In the old days, this would include the ability to play the piano, paint, and sing. Today, it is more common for an "accomplished" person to be crafty, a designer, a gourmet cook and other such modern skills.

Yet, there is something very basic and simple about just accomplishing beautiful things at home. These simple things include doing the laundry, keeping the kitchen clean, making pleasant meals, and being hospitable.

I prefer the simple accomplishments.

These days, it is an amazing feat just to do the basics of homemaking. It is also very difficult when one has a large family, or when one is feeling ill. Sometimes, I do a little baking in the morning, and then I dust and vacuum. I might get some of the laundry started before making lunch. When my grandbabies are here, I am very busy reading to them, playing with them, and making their snacks and meals. I am delighted with these types of accomplishments!

Still, I have to take many breaks. Accomplishing things is tiring. The breaks are necessary. We need to pace ourselves. Even still, there is a special secret to doing great things in the home.

I once read about this little girl who said that when she was holding her grandfather's hand, she could run much faster than she could alone. She was able to do so much more when her grandfather was with her. There was an analogy that this also applies to our Heavenly father. We can only do so much alone. But when we walk close to the Lord, leaning on Him, working with (and for) Him, we can accomplish great and mighty things.

18

A Quiet Little Home Life

I put up some fresh white curtains in the bedroom. Our windows are very large and let in the summer sun. It cheers the room. It was a happy time of housekeeping. It is so quiet here without any noise from a radio, television, or the ringing of the phone. It was the perfect time for morning prayers. This quietness, at the beginning of the day, makes one want to thank and worship the Lord. Hearing the Bible being read by one of the children, and someone taking a turn to pray, is such a beautiful way to start the day.

Then off we go to our own duties. One does school work, yard work, and miscellaneous chores. Another cleans, does laundry, and organizes the rooms. Each of us has our labor, but we do it, mainly with quiet.

When the grandchildren are here with their laughter and mischief, amidst our quiet world, we are more apt to settle into a chair to read them books, sit with them and play their little games, and enjoy the preciousness of their company.

There are certainly times for phone calls, and times to rest while enjoying something on television. But these are moments of recreation which halt the joy of the quiet work, as we putter about the house putting it to right.

In the evening, as we wind down the day, and sit by lamplight, it is time for evening prayers. This is a precious end to a happy time of living a quiet life. We hear natural sounds of the outdoors and the echoes of the birds singing by the window. We say silent prayers of thanksgiving in our hearts. We have a joyful peace that passeth all understanding.

19

In Pursuit of Christian Duty

We spent the last month taking care of Grandfather, and then Nana needed medical care. I have spent an enormous amount of time in Hospitals this winter. When I am home, I clean, do laundry and care for the family. Being busy about the house is a privileged kind of duty that I am grateful for. We have found ways to make the trials a bit of fun. Many mornings, I would sit in the kitchen of the Grandparents, taking notes of the day's plan. Did they need firewood? Dishes washed? Some errands run? We made a plan for dinners. It reminded me of Rose Kennedy, and how she would breakfast at home, ordering dinner from the domestic staff who cared for her family and house.

Some would say that we mothers are being run ragged, by all we have to do in a day. Some would be haggard and worn by such trials and hard work. But as long as there are times of rest, and little homemaking breaks, we can manage beautifully. This is a sweet spirit of Christian duty.

All day long, there are silent praises and prayers uttered up to Heaven. All day long, there is a pleading for strength and courage - and these are gently given.

Many times we Mothers read our Bible in the twilight hours, or in a spare moment, while children are napping, and we delight in a holy communion. We do not seek Christian duty, we do not wonder what God would have us do; we simply make ourselves available for the Master's use and He will fill our time with His glorious work. When we walk in His ways and Love His Laws, we will find Him in the humblest of work. This brings us the greatest joy we will ever experience, this side of Heaven.

20

The Old Song Book

My elementary school required all children to take choir practice. I still remember being in the music room and the teacher conducting the class in song. We each had music sheets and were taught very basic notes. Some of the children, in later years, were in performances during the holidays. They would sing Christmas songs at the local mall. I remember playing the violin on stage during a recital with my class in the school auditorium.

In later years, as teenagers, my sister and I joined our church choir. Our family went to Sunday school, the main service, and then went home for the afternoon. There was an evening service and we always went early because choir practice was one hour before the time of evening worship. We girls learned many songs from the church hymnal. We also went to nursing homes to sing on a monthly basis.

Every Sunday, our small congregation would sing from the hymnal. Someone played the piano and it sounded lovely. We would sing "Softly and Tenderly Jesus is Calling" during the altar call at the end of the service. We sang "Trust and Obey," "Beulah Land," and many more. There were about 15 songs that we would sing on a rotating basis every week. This helped the entire congregation to become familiar with the songs, to love them, and to know them well. Our choir director then taught us "It is Well with My Soul," one of my favorite songs of all time. He explained the story behind the song, which made it so precious to sing and to hear. We rehearsed it many times and then the choir got up in front of the church and sang it to the congregation on a Sunday morning. I know that song so well, because our director was an excellent teacher, that I can sing it without musical accompaniment.

I love those old Church Hymnals so much that when my children were little I was able to buy one book for each of us. We still have them and love to read through the unfamiliar songs, and to sing the ones we know well. I have pages folded and marked for all the ones I know. I sing them to myself or to cheer up the grandbabies.

One afternoon, the babies were fussy, so I put each one in a highchair with some toys. I sat next to them in a kitchen chair with my old songbook and sang them many songs. They listened and played happily for quite some time.

Anytime I am feeling low or worried, I can open up the song book and start singing songs like, "When the Roll is Called up Yonder, I'll Be there," and that cheers me greatly. It makes everything okay.

Mother's Hour

21

The Diary of a Housewife

I watched, "Christmas in Connecticut," with my grandbaby yesterday. The main character wrote a column in a housekeeping magazine. I believe it was in the 1940's. The title of her column was "The Diary of a Housewife." She talked about her New England farmhouse, her baby, her husband, and her cooking. She described the beauty of her home and surroundings. It was a highly popular column. Some of the readers were nurses who lived in hotels and rented rooms. They longed for marriage and a home of their own.

The housewife's diary was important to the public. She described a life that many dreamed of. She made cooking and housekeeping something to aspire to and, I am sure, cheered many fellow housewives along the way.

I keep my own personal diary (or journal). Very often life is so loud and full of trouble, that I am delighted to sit down and write about all the pretty and happy things that happened despite the trials. Somehow I capture the reality of life - the love and the kindness - and this helps me to go on. How would I ever remember how sweet it is when grandbaby sings herself to sleep if all I thought about was how weary I was from pacing the floors with her? I write down these little happenings so I remember the precious and not just what happens behind-the-scenes of the precious. What it takes to have a lovely, peaceful home takes unbearable work and a "with a will" attitude.

To stop and write about the chirping of birds, or how lovely the family looked at the breakfast table, is endearing.

Perhaps we would find more happiness if we kept our own diaries of pleasant thoughts.

Mother's Hour

22

Gracious Homemaking

Early in the morning, I am awakened by a little baby being placed in my arms. It is my grandson. I take care of him in the morning so his mother can get some extra rest. I have given up on the idea of my early morning tea, as the sun rises, while I sit in the parlour. Those kinds of mornings are a distant memory. My hours, days, weeks, months are consumed with the blessing of Christian duty. It happened gradually, my personal time, and my own way, being taken over with something far more precious.

In the quiet of the morning, I am busy with home duties. I tidy the parlour, and start the tea. I make Grandbaby's playpen look inviting. His blanket is neatly folded over the side. I take a little box and fill it with small toys. This is placed in the corner of the pen, along with a few carefully displayed books. When he is brought upstairs by his Mother, he is excited to go in there while we prepare the morning meal.

I visit with the great-grandparents (who live with us) for a few minutes to see how they are doing. I hear the plans for the day and then get back to my own home duties.

My teenage son sits at the table with me, over tea, and we study. I have a stack of large books and have taught him how to use them. We have The Strong's Concordance, the 1828 Webster's Dictionary, Matthew Henry's Commentary, along with our Bibles. We study in the parlour and then he goes off to do his own studies.

Soon I am busy with Grandbaby and his Mother. We cook and clean and smile and laugh. We talk as we work and we watch all the wonderful antics of baby. Another little cherub will be here very soon and we are excited!

I take a little rest in the parlour chair and try to read. I have an afghan and sit near the fire. It is not long before someone calls me away to another part of the house. I am needed for this or that. But I am ready. My book reading is put down at any moment, because I am on-call for the needs of this house.

Afternoon arrives and Grandbaby needs his nap. Portions of this house suddenly become quiet as we get the little one settled to sleep.

The dinner hour is here and we start cooking. There are dishes to do, and laundry to check on. Often someone comes in - whether it is one of my grown children, or Mister, and wants to talk and have a little parlour visit. We take a break from our work to sit for a while.

It is getting late. Grandbaby needs his bath and his bedtime. I visit the great-grandparents again and make sure they are settled for the evening. Then I do the evening chores while listening to old time gospel music on my kitchen radio.

We have evening prayers and a little Bible reading.

When most of the family has gone off to bed, I am back in the kitchen, doing those last minute chores which bring joy to the family - making it all look neat and pleasant.

This is gracious homemaking. It is cheerful work in the home and a kindness in caring for the family.

23

A Cozy Humble Home

I love old houses with their quaint wallpaper and classic designs. These places remind me of the simplicity of family life where Mother is always home. She is there when the children come home from school, work, or play. She is there to comfort them with her great patience and dedication to her family.

In our old house I like to sweep the floors in the evening and turn on the lamps. I straighten up the chairs and make the kitchen and parlour look neat.

There are pretty designs in the old woodwork. I love to polish the banister that goes down the front staircase. The walls are decorated with old paintings. The house cost little and so do its furnishings. It is a *humble home*.

There is nothing of modern design here. It is classic and old fashioned. It is peaceful and pleasant. On these cool autumn days, it is a joy to walk into the house and feel the warmth from our wood stove. This brings a cozy feeling of happiness.

There are many mothers who did not grow up in happy homes. They may not have had a living example of homemaking, of being a beloved wife and mother. Sometimes this has to be found in the examples of extended relatives, neighbors, those in the church, or in old books and other types of uplifting literature.

Often the trials and tribulations of life around us make it very difficult to have a cozy life at home. One must always remember that we must have *a will*, a *determination*, to make our homes what they ought to be. It is up to us to oversee and to do the cleaning. It is up to us to rearrange rooms to make them pleasant. It is up to us to keep our hearts set on things above, through prayer and Bible reading, so that a warmth of holiness strengthens us to do the work of making happy homes.

To have a cozy, humble home is something to strive for. It is something that will take great effort and work, just like our relationships take much labor. The most important ingredient to having a happy home is to have a humble, grateful heart.

24

Despairing Over the Cold

This is the time of year when despairing over the cold is common for me. Last month we ran out of oil to heat part of this large 1800's house. I had an emergency delivery arrive the following morning. It happened again the other night. I was woken up in the middle of the night because there was no heat. It was below zero outside and the temperature was rapidly dropping in the house. I called the oil company first thing in the morning.

That day, the grandbabies and I spent the day in the parlour near the wood pellet stove. We couldn't play in their rooms because it was too cold. The babies were entertained with toys, crayons, snacks and some children's movies. Every now and then, one of us went downstairs to the nursery to get a few more toys. We had to wear a coat; it was so cold in there!

By mid-afternoon, our oil arrived and the heat was turned back on. It took a few hours for the temperature to rise. The despair of being cold turned to joy. It is amazing how the simple comfort of warmth can delight the heart! By the children's bedtime, all was back to normal.

After this ordeal was over I thought about the Pilgrims. They had settled on the coast in a Massachusetts town. Today, a living museum shows visitors the reality of the harshness of their living conditions. Ocean air is bitterly painful and cold in the winter. I cannot imagine how they kept their spirits up to get through the cold!

In my father's boyhood days, everyone used a wood stove for heat. The fire would be allowed to go out when it was bedtime. The children often shared a bed and were covered with homemade quilts. Mothers would also have hot water bottles or warm baked potatoes wrapped up by their feet for the children to give them extra warmth. In the morning, someone would brave the icy cold and start the fire so breakfast could be made and the family would get dressed for the day.

In old remembrance books children wrote of waking up on cold winter nights to find snow had come through the roof and landed on their quilts. They would also get dressed by the kitchen stove because that is the only place in the house where there was warmth. These same children would attend a one room schoolhouse which was heated by a wood stove. The desks would be moved to keep the children as close to that source of heat as possible.

These stories make me realize how very pampered I am. But being warm is one of the greatest needs during a New England winter. Many people spend the year saving for a family vacation, or a shopping spree. We spend our year saving up every dime we can to buy our heat for the winter. I won't even let myself think of what it would be like to visit Hershey, Pennsylvania, Dollywood in Tennessee, or even Disneyland, because as wonderfully enjoyable as those trips would be, I am only able to sit by the wood stove in a rocking chair, reading my Bible, and waiting for the winter to thaw out into a pleasant spring.

25

The Quiet Little World of Home

There was a time, many years ago, when home was a quiet place of seclusion. It was a dream to have one's own home and to rest and be refreshed in that special place for family. In Charles Dickens' "*Great Expectations*" there is a character in the story, who is firm and professional at work, but leaves his "*heart at home.*" He does not talk about his home or his garden to co-workers. His personal life is left at the gate of his own estate, when he takes that long walk into the city each morning. Those at work, or out in the world, do not know about his happy home. It is a place of peace and gentleness.

Home used to be a little world of privacy and rest.

Today, the generation coming up has been exposed to reality programming, constant updates from friends and family about every aspect of their daily life in social media, and are free with pictures, stories, and anecdotes about what goes on in their own life. They not only view all of this, they contribute to it. There is no peace. There is no quiet. There is no time to recover from a tiring world that keeps us all on edge and "riled up."

Little ones, before they went to bed at night, had a gentle routine to get them ready for quiet and rest. They would have a bath and story. In the twilight hours, as the stars shone down through the windows, these little ones would say their prayers and get tucked into bed. They could fall asleep content and comfortable. No one was allowed to "rile" them up or get them over -stimulated before bed. Bedtime was when the day had been wound down and all was quiet and well. This is just what home should be like for all of us. This is what a quiet little world used to be like when a weary soul went home to rest from his vocation in the "city." Home was like the "country;" It was that quiet place where one could "get away from it all."

Some live in apartments, mobile homes, cottages, or great mansions. But once the door of that royal home is closed; (*for all homes can be like places where royalty resides*) it should be a private place where paparazzi is *not welcome;* Even if that paparazzi are the residents of one's own home, releasing stories and photos that should be kept for their own family's happiness. We must try to learn from royal families and those in the public eye, that family deserves a private life. This helps bring peace and security.

Home should be a quiet, happy world where one can truly rest and recover from a loud and stressful world.

26

There Are Scorners Everywhere

There have been many great men in history who have given their time, health, and life to do the Lord's work. They have walked through their lives living the old paths despite scorners and hecklers in the sidelines. In this great country, those scorners were the minority. Today, it seems, in these modern days, there are many more scorners than there are people of great moral character, who openly love their Bibles and live noble lives.

I once saw a documentary of the life of Elvis Presley. He sang old time gospel music with the great quartets like The Blackwood Brothers. Some of these men said they would sing well into the night with him, on their own time, out of the limelight. There was great comfort in singing, and in hearing, of hymns and old gospel music.

Every summer, my Uncle's church hosted week - long revival meetings. He was the preacher. Everyone would get all dressed up, on hot summer evenings, and were so excited to hear his sermons. We sang the old time songs out of the hymnals, and we would be convicted and strengthened by the powerful message. It brought many to tears. By the time these weeks were up, we would all go home refreshed and equipped to seek a godly life, despite the scorners around us.

I have heard it said by many a preacher - "A Christian ought to be happy!" When we have a close walk with the Lord, there is a great feeling of peace and joy in our hearts. There is such joy that even in dark times, we have a bond with the Lord who comforts us and gives us such peace that the world can never know. This peace makes us happy!

The other day, I had a song in my mind, "*I'll Meet You in the Morning*" sung by The Blackwood Brothers. I was searching through my tapes and trying to find the song. I wanted to do some baking in my kitchen while listening to this particular tape. . . This often happens to me. What is familiar to us and what is precious to us, in regards to music or literature, gives us a sort of craving. In this case, it was a craving for good things. Sometimes the body craves a certain food and, we are told, that it is because we need a certain vitamin or nutrient and that causes the craving. This can also happen in spiritual matters. Have you ever had a craving for the sound of "*Amazing Grace*" or "*Peace in the Valley*"? This is a need for a spiritual vitamin to sustain you and to give you courage.

In these days, church attendance is down. Modest dressing is "out of fashion". Purity, kindness, and the beauty of a consecrated life are rare. People today are made fun of for being sober. They are made fun of for following the Ten Commandments. They are ridiculed for being "narrow minded" and "prudish." These slang terms are the world's arrows against those who love the comfort and joy of a godly life.

Do not be weary of prayer meetings, all night gospel singings, tent revival meetings, and the daily time of family worship. This is the old time religion that will quench the cravings of the soul.

Today, more than ever, we need the strength of godliness and holiness so that no heckler can make us stumble. No heckler should be able to distract us or divert us from the most beautiful, happy life they may never know. We must stand strong and continue to love our Bibles, love purity, and love a life of "Amazing Grace." We are on a narrow, difficult path, toward the gates of Heaven. But God's children shall all meet up together "over yonder" on that beautiful shore on the greatest "morning" of all.

27

A House Full of Babies

The house was full of people today. To have family and close friends visiting amidst our domestic duties makes the day go by pleasantly.

We have three little grandbabies here, ages 2 and under. There are routines and schedules to follow but we can all visit and talk and laugh while we work and care for the children.

When it is time for someone's nap, everyone will scatter. The house is kept quiet and peaceful so little ones can get their rest.

Many of our guests help with the work during the day. Some sweep the floor, do the dishes, or hold a baby. We also organize and sort laundry, prepare snacks and meals, and do errands. Someone will say, "Can I get you a snack?" or "Do you need anything before I go upstairs?" The house becomes a lovely place for a flurry of activity and hospitality.

Someone prays with a toddler before meals. I sing hymns while rocking babies to sleep. Someone reads the Bible to me, or recites a beloved passage of Scripture. We pray as needs arise, or as some burden is laid on our heart.

We take care of these wonderful babies, and each other, *gratefully*, knowing our foundation is strong in the Lord.

28

To Earn and Not To Spend

In Colonial days, girls and young ladies were taught diligence and productivity. Some of the things they were trained to do:

1. Cook all the meals, keep a garden, and preserve food.

2. Wash, dry and iron clothing, and do mending to make everything last.

3. They often had a loom in their homes where they would take wool from the sheep and process it into some usable material to make clothes for the family.

4. They were taught embroidery, and cross stitching. Girls would do their needlework in a "sampler" with sayings, proverbs, and poems that had great meaning.

One of the poems presented diligence and hard work in the home, ending with the words:

"To Earn and Not to Spend." *

This reminded me of the book, "*Farmer Boy*" by Laura Ingalls Wilder. The mother was incredibly productive and prudent in her homemaking. She made pies and bread and stews. She made sure her children were washed and clean and that they wore carefully kept clothing. If there was a rip in a shirt or in a dress, she would sew it up, as she sat by the fire in the evenings. Mothers, in those days, had work baskets in the parlour. This is where they would do their handwork after the chores were finished for the day. There was a time for everything and a time for each task. There was order in the home. This was the secret to a comfortable, peaceful life.

These Mothers had abundance from their gardens and they would fill the pantry shelves and root cellars with plenty of food. This cost them nothing but labor. This was part of "earning" and not "spending."

Today, there are many ways we mothers are "spending" money that might not be best.

I used to stock up on (many) large cans of coffee when they were marked down in price, thinking I was saving Mister money. But lately, I have come to realize that this *excessive* inventory was tying up money that was needed for the savings bank. It was needed for "rainy days" and for other needs. It put me into the mode of *always* stocking up on many different things to the point that money was being spent on a monthly basis to "save" rather than taking all that money and putting it into the bank.

The definition of "saving" used to mean putting it aside, not trading it for goods or services.

Today, we are told that we are "saving money" when we buy things. This is part of the problem of we mothers losing our productivity in the home. We are not as diligent in our work of *producing*. We are too busy consuming, buying all kinds of things. We are taught to buy all the time.

I love the simple poem from the old days that urges ladies -

"To Earn and Not to Spend."

These are certainly wise words, from just a simple sampler stitched by young ladies from Colonial days.

From   - Boston Evening - Post, December 10, 1744.

Mother's Hour

29

Thrifty Elegance

Over the summer, Mister and I came across a beautiful plate. It was made in England. At the time, I had been reading through "*Dombey and Son*" by Charles Dickens, and was drawn to the lovely blue and white artwork depicting an 1800's British scene. The plate didn't cost very much, at just a few dollars. Mister encouraged me to buy it. I was delighted. It now sits in a decorative holder in our chambers.

Throughout the years, we have been given pretty things to decorate. Our home has been furnished and designed in an old fashioned way: Here a little and there a little. At times I will wait years before I find just the right item which might go on one of the walls, or perhaps we wait to find the right curtain for a single window in one of the little rooms. (As an example - our bedroom curtains cost only $4 each and are unique in a sheer tan color, bordered with lace.) These are fun and exciting ways to create a

Mother's Hour

charming place to live. It also encourages great patience and gratefulness when we wait to find our treasures.

There is a style, or way of life, called thrifty elegance. It costs very little, sometimes a few dollars. At other times it costs nothing (in the form of hand-me-downs from relatives and friends). We accept just what we need so that our home is not overly crowed with "things." It is a simple, yet pretty way of life to add touches of charm.

This sort of elegance can also come from our manners and our dignity. When we live on a small, fixed income, we can do it with grace and confidence, knowing we use our hard work and abilities to keep a neat and tidy home. We can serve our meals in a classy way. How many of us set a formal dinner table with napkins, real dishes, and serving bowls? This is part of elegance, even if we serve humble food. In this modern day, home cooking is so rare that it is a treat! It is also very frugal.

There is something very beautiful about being a creative homemaker. It takes much time, thought, and effort. We create a restful, pleasant place for our family and our guests when we take the time to create a touch of elegance in a charming home.

30

Life in The Nursery

Several times during the day, I clean the grandchildren's nursery. This is a large playroom full of toys, books, and little rocking chairs. There is a baby gate separating it from one of the larger main rooms. I am often holding Grandbaby while Grandson runs around and plays. I tell him, "let's clean up now." We work together to put the blocks in a special box. Then we stack all the books in a pile. We put the race cars in a row on the toddler desk and set up the toy kitchen. We get everything all in order and ready for playing.

When the room is cluttered with toys scattered all around, it is harder for the children to enjoy the room. We clean as we go. Part of the fun of playing is cleaning. It becomes a normal part of the games. The room is always more exciting when things are freshly put back in order.

Time in the nursery is when characters are formed. It is part of where manners are learned and thinking happens. As the baby plays, I ask him to help me set up some toys. I show him how to create new ideas and I sit nearby while he invents his own games. Through it all, we say, "please" and "thank you." I say to Grandson, "will you help Meme?" I will hand him a small toy that needs to be turned on, or adjusted in some way, and let him do it for me. This naturally teaches him that we all count on him to do important things and he learns pride in a job well done.

Many times Grandson calls out, "I did it, Meme!" He may have cleaned something, built a tower with blocks, or fixed a toy that didn't seem to work. Often, he will get a blanket so I can be warm, or he will offer me a special seat. . . Here a little, and there a little (precept upon precept), the babies learn kindness and goodness as they play and grow in the nursery at home. This is the foundation for a great and godly citizen.

31

Room Service

Years ago, when we owned a country store, we had charming, old rotary phones with an intercom system. There was a phone behind the front counter, one in the back room's commercial kitchen, and one in the upstairs apartment where we lived. The phone line was a business phone connected to the store. It had a delightful intercom system, for our own personal use, that we greatly enjoyed. One of us was always using the intercom to ask for dinner, a snack, or a drink. The building was very big and it would have been difficult to talk to each other in person when we were all over the place, either working in the store, or upstairs doing housework or schoolwork. Our five children were the ones who used the intercom the most. They often called each other and ran around doing their own errands. What fun for them to actually live in a general store and be able to get a snack or drink anytime they wanted!

It has been many years since those days. We live across the street from our old store. We see it every day when we look out the window or drive by on an errand. Here in our 1850's colonial house, we have a "wall" phone unit with an old fashioned cord. To talk on the phone, I would have to sit at the dining room table and not venture too far. Perhaps the cord would reach to the kitchen stove and I could talk for a few minutes while making dinner. Last year, we decided to buy a set of cordless phones. There are two units. I read the manual and realized it had an intercom system similar to the one we had in our store. I was delighted. John and I use the phones here constantly. This house has three stories. We are often all over the place doing a variety of things. Mostly we are taking care of two of my grandbabies. Each day, John (18) takes Grandson out to play. He has a phone with him. He will call me and say, "Is baby's lunch ready?"

Many times I will call and ask for a ginger ale or "would you make me some tea." I am either in the back parlour with Grandbaby, or on the lower floor with both the grandchildren in the nursery.

In the evening, at the children's bedtime, their mother will get settled with them for the night, but always calls on the intercom for a forgotten snack or beverage. We are so used to these calls from each other that we have learned to answer the phone's page by saying, "Room service. What can I get for you?"

Mother's Hour

32

Ruth Graham Called Herself a Happy Housewife

I have been reading from an old book written by Ruth Graham (the late wife of evangelist Billy Graham.) She had five children and was a housewife. She was also the daughter of missionaries and spent part of her childhood in China. Throughout her life, she has been all over the world, but the happiest place, according to her, was to be at home.

She was a loving mother with an incredible sense of humor. She was also a wonderful wife and a great woman of faith and prayer. The example of her life is inspiring.

In her book, "It's My Turn," she shares some family photographs of her sweet family. In other books she wrote, she shares that some of her children had lived for years as Prodigals but are now serving the Lord. So encouraging!

Mrs. Graham was a happy housewife. That does not mean her life was one of ease and perfection. It means that she loved her job as a wife and mother at home. What more could we ever want out of life?

33

Old Cowboy Stories

When I was growing up, children did not have control of the television. If our father was not home, we could watch a program. Often we would watch something in the afternoon, when we got home from school. This was "*The Brady Bunch*" or "*Little House on the Prairie*." But when Dad came home, we got up and did some chores, did our homework, and helped Mother set the table for dinner. In the evening, we cleaned the kitchen, picked up our rooms, and studied. Sometime around 7 in the evening, if we wanted to watch television, we would go into the living room and watch whatever Dad was watching. We knew he worked hard all day and had to rest. We knew we had our turn earlier in the day to watch children's programming. This was the way it was, and we didn't know any other way. We were happy with it. We loved and respected our Father and would not have dreamed of expecting to watch what we wanted all the time.

Mother's Hour

On Saturday mornings, we children often watched cartoons. Then we would go outside to play before starting our chores. During this time, Dad was mowing the lawn, working in the garden, repairing the house, fixing the cars, or doing a project in the garage. He would come in, now and then, for some coffee or iced tea. He took very short breaks and then went back to his chores. In the early afternoon, he would stop to have his lunch, and then he would rest in the recliner to watch Cowboy shows. This was a wonderful time. I often sat in there with him and watched it too. These were old programs with good guys and bad ones. Recently I came across some DVDs Dad had given us. They are called, "*The Guns of Will Sonnet.*" This was a television series which was broadcast during the 1960's. It was about a Grandfather gunman with his grown grandson. They traveled through western towns on horseback, searching for the Grandson's father. In each town they passed through, there was always some kind of trouble going on where they stepped in to help. The wisdom and the lessons were wonderful. These men were the "good guys" and were admirable. They were good men who protected and upheld justice. At the end of every episode, we see the men on horseback traveling to another town, continuing their search. And while they ride, we hear the voice of Grandpa, saying a heartfelt prayer; talking to the Lord with great faith and devotion, thanking Him for keeping them safe.

Mother's Hour

These old cowboy stories that I grew up watching with my father are endearing and nostalgic. I am delighted to have found this set and am happy to let my teenagers watch them. When my boys were little, I bought them red cowboy hats and "Will Rogers" Guitars. I remember once hearing that the movie "*Shane*" had incredible lessons for young men. We girls would do well to see this kind of character and nobility in gentleman. We need to see men who have great manners towards girls and who will protect them. We need to see more "good guys" who will not stand by and let evil happen. The old Cowboys are like a legend on the screen to teach us something we rarely get to see in these modern days.

34

An Ordinary Life at Home

Most housewives used to rise very early in the morning. They would do the wash and then go out into the fresh air, in the quiet of the day, to hang the clothes on the line. This was a peaceful work. This was a time when they could pray, praise the Lord for his goodness, and enjoy some little moments of solitude.

A Homemaker would spend time in the kitchen, making a homemade breakfast, standing near the kitchen window doing dishes and making home a pretty place to be.

Sweeping, washing floors, dusting furniture, folding laundry, and making home pleasant and comfortable brought joy to grateful hearts.

Mother would read the Bible and pray. She would do mostly the same things each day. The routine brought stability and comfort to

Mother's Hour

the family. Most everyone had the same kind of home - an ordinary home - where Mother was home and she took care of housekeeping.

This quiet life was like living out in the country during a winter holiday. It was like the days when there were horses and buggies, and travelling was not common before automobiles became the normal mode of transportation. Staying at home, tending the home, caring for the family, and helping others was ordinary.

This type of life is what the current generation is missing. They are starving for something they have never personally experienced. They are used to technology, multi-tasking, entitlement, self-absorption, and the frantic pace of the constant bombardment of modern advertising.

An ordinary life at home is one of the greatest needs of our time. We need mothers who will peacefully tend the home and genuinely love to be there. They need to be brave and patient. They need tender hearts and self-less spirits. The keeper of these ordinary homes are best found among those who are on their knees in prayer, and in those who find their greatest joy in reading the Holy Scriptures.

35

Playing House in Real Life

I spend every waking moment caring for two of my grandbabies. Their every smile is my joy. Their falls and spills are my opportunity to comfort and encourage them. They brighten a room with their adorable presence.

When the infant cries, the toddler comforts her. I love to see how much they love and care about each other. I love to sit in the big chair, in the nursery corner, and read piles of books with them. They mostly point to pictures and repeat some of my words. They are learning.

I prepare bottles for baby, and simple lunches and snacks for the toddler. I dress them in their blanket sleepers after baths, and dress them in their nicest clothes for an outing. We are home, here at the Estate, for most of the time and it is a peaceful, happy place to be.

Sometimes there is crankiness or will-full moments of temper, but we soothe them with our patient understanding and kindness. I have many helpers here.

I love that someone else makes my lunch, or brings me tea so I can "Play house" with the babies. I love that I have others to do some of my chores so I am free to sing lullabies and rock in the old chair with a baby.

I also love to do some of the cleaning while holding a baby. One morning I had to vacuum the downstairs carpet, and the toddler got his toy push mower and "vacuumed" along with me. I tell him we are "cleaning the mess." He thinks this is part of our daily routine and is entertained.

Many of us had dolls when we were little girls. We would have doll blankets and clothes and little beds. We would keep our rooms neat and care for our "babies." We did this so lovingly and patiently. This is what it feels like, now, as I get to care for these precious children. Yet, when I notice myself getting overtired or overwhelmed, I pick up one of the cherubs and kiss a chubby cheek and tell the baby what wonderful fun we are going to have in the nursery, and we go and play as if we have all the time in the world.

Mother's Hour

36

The Secret to a Clean House

I have been in many homes and noticed a contrast between lovely surroundings and overwhelming messes. I realize it is very hard to keep a home clean. I realize we are busy and tired. Having a house full of family would seem to make it even more difficult. Some seem to take the approach of taking several hours, one day a week, to really clean a piled up mess. Some, with small children, get a babysitter so they can do the cleaning. What I would like to share with you today are some "secrets" to having a clean house.

Here is the most important, *little known*, secret:

We don't clean a house because it is messy. We clean a house so it doesn't *become* messy.

Here are the tips:

1. To cut down on the spider population, you must regularly sweep and vacuum baseboards, corners and ceilings. (Daily or weekly)

2. To keep a clean kitchen, shortly after a meal, do the dishes. Do them right away.

In my childhood days, we would sit at the dinner table after a meal. Our parents would go into the living room for coffee and to watch the news. We children (one or two of us) would then immediately do the dishes, wash the counters and table, and sweep the floor. *We did not leave the kitchen, after a meal, until the kitchen was clean.*

If you wait to do the dishes, everything gets hardened and it is much more difficult to clean. It is also overwhelming and unpleasant.

3. Make the beds each morning. Fix the sheets, fluff the pillows, and neatly pull the blankets up over the pillows. Make it look neat and pretty. This creates a nice atmosphere in the bedrooms.

4. Do the laundry at regular times. If you have to go to a Laundromat, don't leave until your clothes are completely dried, folded, and placed in a basket. Always fold them and put them away. Make time to do this. Schedule your day around when the dryer is going to stop. This is an efficient part of keeping a nice home.

Mother's Hour

5. If there is a spill (of food, drink, or crumbs), clean it up immediately. This is a safety issue. Even restaurants, stores, and businesses have this policy of immediate care. If left untended, it could damage your property. Or someone could accidentally step in it and track it all over the place. This makes it even more difficult and time consuming to clean.

6. Pass the time (with small children) by cleaning together. Most families color, paint, and do crafts with preschoolers. There is certainly a time for artistic endeavors. But don't ignore the fun and educational opportunities in cleaning, *as a game,* with little ones.

For example: If you are spending an hour taking care of a 4 year old, get a basket of laundry and each of you get a clean facecloth. Step by step (with smiles and encouragement) teach the child to fold. You fold it over once and say, "your turn!" Then watch as the child copies your action. Repeat until at least a few items are folded. Next, start picking up books and saying, "let's put these on the shelf, will you help me?" Or, (to put toys away) help sort different items into little bins (perhaps by object or color).

In daily life, involve your children in the chores by *happily* and *willingly* cleaning together each day. This is how the work gets done!

The children will love spending this time with you and go along with the cleaning. In this way, children are learning, and having fun, while important work is being accomplished.

7. Here a little and there a little. That is the secret approach to keeping the home neat. You pick things up as you go about your day at home. You neaten a room when you walk into it. You do not sit and rest when things are in chaos. You do the work - you do the duty. Then the reward is to sit in the pretty room and take a break.

Now remember the most important secret of all, because it is a pleasant and happy way to clean. And that is to clean as you go along. Clean the house in a way that prevents messes. Make it a joyful part of your daily routine - to clean and to bless those around you by your cheerful efforts.

37

Rededicate the Home

There is a special holiday which comes every week in our home. It is the Sabbath. We anticipate its joy and rest, as the weekdays pass.

Late yesterday afternoon, I put out my best tablecloth. (I only have one - gentle smiles). It is a bit raggedy but a pure white. I have had it for many years and only use it on this special occasion. Then I placed two white candles on the table. These were a gift from one of the children. I never light them. I just put them in their candlesticks and enjoy them as part of "the sign," or "signal" to our family that it is the Sabbath.

Next, I laid out a beautiful china teapot on the side table. This was a recent birthday gift from one of my children. It looked elegant. I then set out to bake a lemon cake.

Mother's Hour

I put out a small vanilla scented candle on the table and lit it. I said a prayer and then went to get the little ones. The sun had not yet set.

I carried Grandson into the room slowly. His eyes lit up at the sight. He hugged me close and said, "*Wow, Meme!*" I told him that this is the Sabbath!

Little Grandbaby was getting fussy. I put each baby in a highchair with some toys. Their chairs are in the adjoining parlour. I faced them towards me so we could talk and laugh while I did my kitchen work.

I got up a little dinner and finished baking the cake. The sun was down. As I went about the serving of the food and the calling of all to the evening meal, I thought about how we take little steps towards holiness and how much it lights a fire of warmth within us.

It was like we had just cleared the home of worldly thoughts, troubles, and stress. We set about to keep the Sabbath and rededicated our home to Holiness. This will strengthen our faith and our walk and will spread to all areas of our lives.

In December there is the "Feast of Dedication," [John 10:22] or "Chanukkah." It is the remembrance of the miracle of lights and the reclamation of the holy Temple to the service of God. It has profound and rich meaning.

Mother's Hour

One of the main things I often tell my children is that no matter what the Greeks were doing at that time (the way they were living), the Jewish people would not forsake God's commandments. They continued to live for the Lord. When they reclaimed the Temple, which had been desecrated, they restored it, and relit the menorah. Sometimes, I have older children who make mistakes that cause themselves great pain. I remind them of Chanukkah. I tell them to cleanse the mess in their lives, and restore their lives in the service of God.

We can do this in our homes each day. We can rededicate our lives and our homes. We can do this on the Sabbath, or at any time we feel like we are falling off the path.

Last night, as my grandbabies watched me serve dinner with a peaceful smile, they were content. We enjoyed the beautiful tablecloth and candles. We enjoyed the cake and the happy evening. There was a sense of awe and wonder that this was the Lord's special day and we made the effort towards holiness.

The children see this..... They will remember how Mother dedicated the Home to the Lord.

38

Blessed By the Morning Kitchen Work

I wanted to make a nice batch of banana muffins this morning. There was an old gospel song in my head and I started looking for a CD. The song was by an old southern quartet "The Inspirations" called, "*When I wake up to Sleep No More.*" I was delighted when I managed to find it among some old tapes that my father had made for me, with his gentle handwriting on the outer paper. It says, "For Sharon - gospel singing - The Inspirations."

This tape went on my kitchen radio near the back window. It is raining and dark this morning and the wind is blowing the curtains. Oh, how I love the sounds of old gospel music that is familiar to me. My father had sung many of these songs in our childhood home on weekend mornings as he puttered around the house doing projects or making something in the kitchen.

Mother's Hour

As I busily labored over the complicated recipe for my special muffins, my back started to hurt, but there was great joy in my heart as song after song of heavenly peace echoed through my kitchen.

I thought of heaven and all the work I am doing to "occupy" in the will of the Lord, and in the Lord's work, as a guard and keeper of this home. Soon I heard the old song, "*Is that footsteps that I hear?*" Which talks about heavenly footsteps walking towards us getting ready to sound the trumpet to call us home!

Some may focus their time and energy on great riches, and the exciting world of money or travelling to foreign lands and distant cities. Some may focus on climbing corporate ladders, or getting great fame, or accomplishing amazing things. But this old New England housewife is doing a quiet work of seeking holiness and making home a godly haven, following the lighted path my father lit for me, to follow him to the heavenly gates.

Mother's Hour

39

The Years of Barrenness Healed

When I was pregnant with my fifth baby, 18 years ago, I was diagnosed with cancer. It was a devastating time that ended up leaving me infertile. Many said to me, "well, you have been blessed with five children. That is plenty. Why can't you just be thankful for that?" I realize they were just trying to comfort me. My years of mourning had to be private because few understood my pain.

In Scripture, it was sometimes considered a curse or a punishment when no babies were given. I have been told that old - time Jewish women, during their monthly cycle, mourned when a pregnancy did not occur. We've read of dear Hannah and Rachel who cried out in sorrow, dearly wanting babies. Children are a blessing and a joy to every family. Babies are a precious gift from the Lord.

Mother's Hour

For fifteen years, I cried out for children. I waited on God and begged for mercy. While I have dearly loved, cherished, and cared for the ones I have been given, I have also prayed for healing and for precious souls to be added to our family.

Three years ago, grandchildren started arriving into our Estate. Mister and I now have five grandchildren with two more expected early next year. Our family's barrenness has been healed. Our household, of The White family, is being blessed again with precious and beloved babies.

I am remembering all the pretty clothes, layette sets, crocheted bonnets, sweaters, and booties that my own babies wore. I gave them away, not thinking about the future. What my first and second children wore was given away. New things were obtained for the rest of the children. These too, were later given away. Right now, I should have a trunk holding the best of my babies' clothing to use for the new babies arriving into our family. It used to be that mothers saved baby and toddler clothes for the coming generations. Mothers and grandmothers would mend and care for the clothes and save the best which they knew would last through many more children. They expected more babies to come!

I dearly wish we were not such a throw-away society. I wish we had more faith and a stronger desire for precious children to have in our families. I realize that babies and children are a tremendous amount of work. But what many see as work, I see as a privilege and a joy. This is what a mother is for – this is a mother of nations. It is a serious and amazing job, to raise up precious souls for the Lord.

An empty, clean house without the echo of little footsteps and laughter is a lonely barren house. Let us pray and beg God for children to fill our hearts and lives – and to raise them as lights of holiness to bless this earth and our heavenly home.

40

You Have Three Minutes

During a quick homemaking break, I was reading this book about Billy Graham. There was a large picture of him with his wife. They were in their elderly years and looked so sweet in their home, by the fire.

A quote from Billy said, "Ruth and I were called by God as a team. She urged me to go, saying, 'God has given you the gift of an evangelist. I'll back you. I'll rear the children and you travel and preach.' . . . I'd come home and she had everything so organized and so calmed down that they all seemed to love me. But that was because she taught them to."

I have been thinking about this for days. I was thinking about all the Christian homes that seem crippled because perhaps the husband is not living for the Lord. The entire household may not be all out for God's work. And this can make many of we mothers feel like we are not as important as Billy and Ruth. We may think that if our husbands are not pastors or evangelists or missionaries, that we cannot do as well as Ruth did.

But we have to accept that each of us is unique and made for a purpose. The very hairs of our heads are numbered! God needs us for a certain work. And do you know what? It is the same work that Ruth has always done. Her example of keeping the home and standing behind her husband is invaluable. She has believed in her husband and taken seriously her work of building up the family and inspiring them by her own devotion to the Lord.

We mothers are so very busy, particularly when there are babies and young children in the house. I am helping to raise two of my grandbabies. I know how time consuming the simple task of caring for little ones can be. There is very little time to do basic things like cooking and cleaning.

So whenever I have a few minutes, perhaps I just got Miss Grandbaby (the 7 week old) to finally fall asleep for 10 minutes, I do a little work. I may read something from the Bible. Or I may do a little housework. Often, one can see me rushing about (as if I am on some fun errand here at home), getting myself a pretty cup and putting ice cubes and ginger ale in it. I place it on a little table beside my parlour chair. Next, I will get a tea plate and fix a small lunch for myself, cover it with plastic wrap, and put it near my beverage. Of course, there is not much time to eat, so I have it ready for when the children are settled.

Today, I finally got to sit down. I have Connie Hultquist's book, "*Dear Kitchen Saints*," on a little table nearby and I read from it here and there. My 21 year old son walked in the room. "Hi Mom," he said quietly. "What are you doing?" I sipped on my ginger ale and said, "I am on a lunch break." He smiled and teased me, "A break from what? Being a Mother?" He is adorable. I said, "It is a homemaking break."

Late this morning, the mother of my grandbabies was rocking the youngest baby and said, "You have three minutes, Mom. And then I have to go." She was on her way out and I was to babysit.

What did I do with those minutes? I thought, maybe I should lie down, or get a snack. Or maybe I should do some dishes. But only three minutes? I decided to make my bed. It made the room look more comfortable and pleasant for the day. It made me happy.

Mother's Hour

Three minutes to read the Bible, clean the house, or say a prayer. If we are given those little glimpses of time, we can use them in amazing ways throughout the day. We can do what Ruth did for her husband. We can make home a holy, comfortable place for our families. What better way of redeeming the time?

41

Dishes That Do Not Match

Over the years I have had all kinds of dishes. My favorites are the ones that came from the supermarket. They used to have beautiful china. You could get a tea cup or dinner plate for a small price with your grocery order. Or, sometimes, you would earn stamps from your purchases and could redeem them for free pieces of china. This has always been a fun way to build up a collection of dishes.

When we children were little, my Mother and Aunt each had a favorite pattern from Pfaltzgraff. Each year for birthday or Christmas, they would buy each other a piece to go with their collection. Some years they would get a serving bowl. Another year they would get a dinner platter. They would get a sugar and creamer set and salt and pepper shakers. Piece by piece, year by year, they built up a set of beautiful dishes for their own homes.

Mother's Hour

Last month, at Thanksgiving, I served dinner on dishes that do not match. I loved it! Some of the plates had been a gift from my Mother. Others were gifts from the children. Some were of a special design that I had bought years ago. My dishes are a collection that came over years of homemaking. None of them are expensive, but all are treasured.

Just like my mismatched dishes, my kitchen chairs do not match. Much of my furniture is gathered from a variety of sources - a hand-me-down, a castoff, used furniture store purchase, or something homemade.

It is a humble home we have here, created through love and service. We make the most of what we have and are grateful.

Mother's Hour

42

Putting Papa First

Both my grandbabies are napping. It is an ordeal to get them both to sleep at the same time, and is like playing a game of musical chairs. They are in different rooms, so as not to wake up the other one. Of course, having babies in the house again is reminding me of how much Mister needs peace and quiet to survive.

It can get tense when the occasional fit is thrown by Grandson (the toddler), or Miss Grandbaby (7 weeks) is impatient for her bottle. But I sing to them and talk sweetly to them. I also have help from one of the Uncles for part of the day. There is noise, of course, while we get them settled down. The noise is only for a little while, and then the smiles of contentment and rest come to their little faces.

Mother's Hour

Crying babies and settling down children is a grand work for mothers. If we have nothing else taking up our time, or trying to drag us away from the joy of home, we can patiently and peacefully do this work. But Mister, like all men, must work out in the world. He hears noise and is bombarded with all kinds of disruptions. So I have to make a little extra effort to make sure Mister (or "Papa" to the babies) is comfortable and happy.

To do this, I make sure he is happy in one of the pretty rooms, here at the Estate. I make sure the window is open so he gets a cool spring breeze. The chirping birds, sound of the rushing river, and his television are just what he needs to rest for a while. He rests while I get the babies settled.

Papa spends much of his days with babies. Grandson's face lights up when his grandfather walks into a room. He calls out, "My Papa!" And runs to him. And little Grandgirl is comforted by his voice.

Since the babies love Papa so much, and he is so good with them, I sometimes forget that Papa needs times of rest. I forget that Papa also spends time out in the hectic world earning the living. I forget that Papa needs time for quiet and peace. He cannot calmly keep up with the pace I do, here at home.

Putting Papa first is something I have to constantly remind myself. I don't want him to get overburdened and overstressed. So I have to remember to smile at him more. I need to ask, "Can I get you something to drink?" or, "Would you like to watch a little television for awhile?" Sometimes, he will be so busy mowing our two acres, or repairing something, that he forgets to stop and recover. If I don't remind him, and there is a little chaos indoors, he gets overstressed and this affects the happiness in our home.

Women of today don't understand what it takes to keep a peaceful home. Part of the job includes taking care of a husband and making sure he has a little respect and quiet.

There are little ways we can do this. It used to be that Dad had his own chair. It was a recliner or some comfortable seat. The children were not to sit there. Dad also had his place at the table. He was served first. This was not because he demanded it, and certainly not because he was selfish, it was simply a way of showing honor to the head of the family.

I was watching part of an old movie the other day. It was "How Green Was My Valley." It depicted a normal family where the women were home cooking and cleaning and all the men were out working. When Dad and his older boys came home from work, Mom and the daughter made sure they had soap and water to wash up, a towel to dry, and a hot meal on the table for supper. The narrator described their life by saying, "Dad was the head of the house, and Mom was its heart."

We mothers have the compassion and the nurturing love which allows us to take care of our family. In this modern day of broken marriages and hurting homes, we ought to make that extra effort to put all the "Papas" first.

Mother's Hour

43

Listening For Mister's Cane

My husband is recovering from an accident. I ride with him to his medical appointments, and do my best to make sure he has the food and rest he needs. Here at home, I keep busy with cooking, cleaning, and projects. I am often in the back parlour reading a book or in the kitchen doing some necessary chore. Today I swept the front porch and walked the grounds, looking at all the colorful wildflowers on the property. I keep busy in a quiet way. I want everything to be peaceful so Mister can get his rest. Throughout the day, I drop what I am doing to check on him. I put down my book, or stop washing the dishes. I do this especially when I hear him moving about the house. I want to make sure he is not hurt, or that he has what he needs.

The other day he had a doctor's appointment. Before we got out of the car, Mister reached for his cane. I walked beside him at a very slow pace. His step is very slow and is a struggle. I walk with him into the building and then he kindly tells me to sit in the lounge while he checks in. This is his small way of trying to take care of me. This man used to open doors for me, carry my packages, and treat me like a fragile and gracious lady. His kind treatment of me inspires me to meekness, gentleness, and a compassion for others.

I waited for him in the lounge, reading a book, while he was in with the medical staff. Every so often, I would hear a noise. This would cause me to pause, look up, look around, and see if Mister was in the doorway. I did this at every sudden noise. I was waiting for Mister, listening for the sound of his cane on the floor. I knew that once he stepped through the door, he would glance my way across the room and nod for me to go. I knew that he was in terrible pain and I didn't want him to suffer any more than necessary. This meant that I had to listen for him, pull myself away from a Dickens' novel I was absorbed in, and happily and cheerfully get up to take care of my husband.

After quite some time, Mister appeared, and I quickly got up. I walked beside him, at his pace, while he told me about his medical progress. Then we got into the car and drove home.

Mother's Hour

My listening for Mister's cane, at the doctor's that day, reminded me of a servant's heart and how we wait for the sound of our Master's Heavenly footsteps. We are to do our work here in this world, while constantly pausing; looking up to see if the time is near to go to our Heavenly home.

44

The Old Country

Many Immigrants who came to America had left a special culture behind. It was a place of industry, cleanliness, morality, modesty, and great faith in God. They had many like minded neighbors and family who lived just as they did. When they arrived in the States, there were sort of ghettos where different groups lived among one another – the Irish with the Irish, the Italians with the Italians, Jewish with Jewish, etc. They were able to keep some of the old country alive in this way, because they had the same traditions and values. But their children started to assimilate into the new "modern" world. They were embarrassed that Mama wore shawls and long dresses. They were embarrassed by their parent's accents. They were embarrassed by many things from the old country as they noticed it was ridiculed by their peers in the schools and places of work.

"The Old Country," to the parents, was their beloved homeland and they loved their faith and values. It was HOME to them. And even though these people were often told to *"get with the times"* and *"this is a new world, it is time to get modern,"* they did not change their old fashioned ways.

It has been said by many that their Mamas never seemed to sleep. They were industrious in the home, mending and making clothes, baking, cleaning, doing the wash, and caring for the family and visitors. Little ones would go to bed at night, hearing the quiet sound of Mama doing her mending by the fireside. They would wake up in the morning to her preparing for breakfast in the kitchen. Children felt comforted knowing that if they awoke in fear, or sickness, during the night, that Mama was always there to take care of them. They felt safe with a Mother like that – a Mother from the old country who dedicated her life to her home and family.

Many of these mothers would sing beautiful hymns and godly songs in their native language as they worked around the home. They would sing these as lullabies as they rocked babies and tucked children into bed. These mothers would pray for every little thing and praise and thank God throughout the day. The children were in awe of Mama's faith.

These Immigrant Mothers taught their children duty in the home, giving them daily work, having them help with whatever housekeeping was to be done each day. The children had set times for meals and rest – baths and bed. They had order and cleanliness from these mothers of "the old country." This was an old fashioned upbringing from another time.

Today, there are hundreds of options for entertainment, recreation, food, and leisure. There is a lot of confusion about how to raise our children, and the mistaken idea that we must make their childhoods "easier" with more "fun" and "leisure" than the last generation. This causes great distraction and laziness in our youth. What is being lost is the work ethic, the *gratefulness*, and the most wonderful pure faith in a mighty God.

After our trials and troubles in the world, we should long for the day when we can go to the new world of old fashioned values and beautiful morality. We long for the old homeland. This is where we are headed. It is a longing for "The Old Country" in Heaven.

Mother's Hour

About the Author

Mrs. White is a housewife of more than a quarter of a century, a beloved mother of five children, and a grandmother of five. She is the granddaughter of revival preacher, LD Murphy. She lives with her family in an 1800's house in rural Vermont.

For more information or to find Mrs. White's books, please visit:

The Legacy of Home Press

http://thelegacyofhomepress.blogspot.com

Also see Mrs. White's blog:

http://thelegacyofhome.blogspot.com

Mother's Hour

52438962R00072

Made in the USA
Lexington, KY
29 May 2016